KU-277-051

FORD HOUSE
LIBRARY

HISTORY & TECHNIQUES OF THE
Great Masters

RENOIR

HISTORY & TECHNIQUES OF THE

Great Masters

RENOIR

Guy Jennings

Eagle
Editions

A QUANTUM BOOK

Published by Eagle Editions Ltd.
11 Heathfield
Royston
Hertfordshire SG8 5BW

Copyright © MCMLXXXVIII
Quarto Publishing plc

This edition printed 2002

All rights reserved.
This book is protected by copyright. No part of
it may be reproduced, stored in a retrieval
system, or transmitted in any form or by any
means, without the prior permission in writing
of the Publisher, nor be otherwise circulated in
any form of binding or cover other than that in
which it is published and without a similar
condition including this condition being
imposed on the subsequent publisher.

ISBN 1-86160-469-6

QUMREN

This book is produced by
Quantum Publishing Ltd.
6 Blundell Street
London N7 9BH

Printed in China by
Leefung-Asco Printers Ltd.

CONTENTS

INTRODUCTION
— 6 —

CHRONOLOGY
— 14 —

THE PAINTINGS

LA GRENOUILLERE
— 16 —

THE BOX AT THE THEATER
— 20 —

THE DANCER
— 24 —

BALL AT THE MOULIN DE LA GALETTE
— 28 —

THE SWING
— 34 —

MME CHARPENTIER AND HER CHILDREN
— 38 —

THE UMBRELLAS
— 42 —

THE BATHERS
— 46 —

GIRLS AT THE PIANO
— 50 —

PORTRAIT OF MISIA
— 54 —

LES GRANDES BAIGNEUSES
— 58 —

INDEX
— 62 —

ACKNOWLEDGEMENTS
— 64 —

INTRODUCTION

PIERRE-AUGUSTE RENOIR
Self-portrait
1876
Fogg Art Museum, Cambridge,
Mass.

Late nineteenth-century France witnessed the flowering of a school of painting which, although initially derided, is now probably the best known and most loved in the entire history of art. The group of painters who became known as the Impressionists, rejecting the traditional, old-fashioned and established standards set by the Ecole des Beaux Arts, began the process of turning the world of art and aesthetics on its head which continued until the emergence of a school of truly modern painters by the end of the century. Artists such as Edouard Manet, Edgar Degas, Claude Monet, Alfred Sisley, Camille Pissarro and Pierre-Auguste Renoir each in their own way contributed to a change in technique, subject matter and handling that paved the way for a new understanding of art and its aims.

Of all these painters Pierre-Auguste Renoir is perhaps the most familiar and in many ways the most readily appreciated, but in other ways he is also less easy to understand than some of his contemporaries, and his pictures less straightforward than they often appear. Renoir, although rightly classified as an Impressionist painter, indeed sometimes seen as one of the driving forces in the development of the movement, does not in truth fit easily into it. Landscape does not dominate his work as it does that of Sisley, nor did he share either Monet's fascination with the ever-changing effects of light and weather or Pissarro's concern for experimentation with form, light and the human figure within the landscape. Renoir, like Degas and Manet, was a painter close to Impressionism but never quite of it. He borrowed many of the techniques of the new younger artists, such as the lighter preparations and the stronger, brighter palette, but for much of his subject matter and inspiration he had more in common with the artists of the eighteenth century than with those of the late nineteenth.

The early years 1841-1868

Pierre-Auguste Renoir was born on February 25, 1841,

son of Léonard Renoir, a tailor of modest means in the city of Limoges in the south-west of France. In 1844, the Renoir family moved to Paris in search of a better living and settled in the rue d'Argenteuil in the centre of Paris not far from the Louvre, and it was here, in the shadow of the great museum, that the young Renoir grew up. He was a happy child with a sunny disposition; a spontaneous talker, who made friends easily, and his uncomplicated attitude to life was later to be reflected in the warmth and gaiety of his paintings. Although poor for much of his life, he would never accept lack of money as a barrier to success or to a happy life, and one of his favourite maxims in later life, "there are no poor people," seems to express a refusal to acknowledge poverty of means as a justification for poverty of spirit or imagination.

As a child in school Renoir showed a natural inclination towards scribbling and drawing, but in early life his greater talent appeared to be for singing, and he was for a time a pupil of the composer Charles Gounod, then choir-master at the Church of St Roch in Renoir's neighbourhood. Gounod tried to encourage Renoir's parents to let him follow a musical career, but owing to their poor background (their circumstances had not been improved by the move to Paris), it was necessary for the boy to leave school at the age of thirteen and discontinue his music lessons. Instead, because of his facility for drawing, he was apprenticed as a porcelain painter with the aim of one day decorating the porcelain at the great Sèvres factory on the outskirts of Paris. He quickly displayed a ready talent for his new occupation, but frequently tired of the monotonous subject matter, and would escape into the galleries of the Louvre. Here he could look at the works of the Old Masters, and more particularly those of the great eighteenth-century French painters Fragonard and Boucher, who delighted in depicting the human figure amidst rich and splendid surroundings.

JEAN HONORE FRAGONARD
The Bathers
c.1760
Louvre, Paris

Fragonard's work had been much admired by Renoir ever since his first visit to the Louvre as a young boy. Throughout his life he continued to be inspired by the imagery and subject matter of the eighteenth century, and in particular by the delicacy and opulence of Fragonard's paintings.

The master of the porcelain factory soon recognized his young apprentice's talent, and told his parents that he was too good to be restricted to porcelain painting and should be encouraged to train properly as a painter. In the nineteenth century there were very strict rules regulating art training, and Renoir accordingly began to take lessons to prepare for his entry into the Ecole des Beaux Arts. For a time he continued to maintain himself by porcelain painting, but in 1858 the factory adopted new mechanical reproduction processes, and he was left without employment and had to turn to decorating window blinds, fans and various domestic goods in order to continue his studies. His erstwhile employer's encouragement had strengthened his determination to make his career as a painter, and he spent many hours in the Louvre copying the works of the Old Masters, a traditional part of an aspiring artist's training at the time. One of his favourite works was Boucher's *Diana at the Bath*, a subject which was later to reappear frequently in his own paintings.

By 1862 he had saved sufficient money to enable him to study full-time. He enrolled at the Ecole des Beaux Arts and at the same time entered the studio of Charles Gleyre, chosen because Gleyre was more tolerant of modern ideas than some of the more traditional masters and also because he made only a small charge to cover the cost of his pupils' materials. Here Renoir met three painters who were to have an important influence on him — Claude Monet, Frédéric Bazille and Alfred Sisley. Monet had already been introduced to open-air painting by Eugène Boudin and the Dutch painter Jongkind, and in 1864, at Monet's suggestion, the four young artists began to make painting trips to the forest of Fontainebleau, a favorite haunt of the Barbizon school of painters. Renoir, somewhat easily led by his more dynamic friends, was not immediately taken with the idea of painting out of doors, but was carried along by Monet's infectious enthusiasm. Much of his work at this time is sombre and dark, with too heavy a reliance on the use of bitumen, but he gradually began to lighten his palette, particularly after meeting the landscape painter Narcisse Virgile Diaz de la Peña, one of the Barbizon group,

PIERRE-AUGUSTE RENOIR
Diana
1867
National Gallery of Art, Washington

Like all aspiring artists at the time, Renoir was anxious to gain acceptance at the Salon, and for this work, submitted but rejected, he has chosen a deliberately conservative and classical subject. The handling, however, is more modern, and the influence of Courbet can be seen both in the thick paint, applied with the palette knife, and in the light, airy background landscape.

who encouraged Renoir, advised him against the use of black, and was generous enough to let him buy materials on his own account. Renoir was frequently too poor to buy them himself, and throughout the 1860s, in order to make a living, he would take any commissions that came his way, which sometimes meant such humble tasks as decorating a cupboard or doing small caricatures.

In 1865 Renoir returned to Fontainebleau in the company of Sisley, and met Pissarro and Gustave Courbet, who was an influence on his early work. The young painters had by now left Gleyre's studio, which closed shortly afterwards, and were trying to make their own way in the world, and in 1865 Renoir attempted unsuccessfully to win selection for the Salon with a landscape, entering himself as a pupil of Courbet. Later, after seeing Manet's work, he tried to escape from the earlier influence; Courbet's dark colours and heavy use of the palette knife no longer seemed to offer the possibilities of delicacy of touch that was to become such an important feature of Renoir's work.

The summer of 1868 was spent in Paris, with the city providing the subject matter for several important works, one being *The Pont des Arts*, which clearly shows the influence of Monet and the first traces of the style that would come to be known as Impressionism. During this period Renoir was able to live with Bazille and share his studio; Bazille came from a well-to-do bourgeois family in Montpellier in the south of France, and was able to help both Monet and Renoir. He and Renoir became firm friends and painted each other several times. These were difficult times for Renoir: in spite of Bazille's generosity, he could not even afford to stay in Paris, and was forced to go to his parents, who had retired to Ville d'Avray. He said later, "I would several times have given up if Monet had not reassured me with a slap on the back."

But in spite of hardship, whenever they had enough money to buy materials, Renoir and Monet would paint together like men possessed of a great secret, working along the banks of the Seine in the new suburbs growing up on the edge of Paris at Chatou and Argenteuil. They often painted the same subject, for instance both executed versions of *La Grenouillère*, the name of a bathing and boating resort frequented by fashionable Parisians, and it was here that both painted what are now regarded as the first Impressionist pictures (see page 17).

Changing techniques

As the Industrial Revolution gathered pace various technical innovations were made in the nature and prepara-

tion of paints and canvas, and these, together with the emergence of photography, were to be important influences on the development of Impressionism. The first crucial technical development was that of ready ground and mixed paints in metal tubes, which meant that the artist no longer had to go through laborious work before he was ready to paint. Previously, painters had had to grind their paints by hand with a pestle and mortar and then prepare them for painting by adding oil, usually linseed oil. This was a long process which could only be carried out in the studio, thus effectively ruling out the use of oil paint out of doors for any but the smallest and thinnest of sketches. The development of ready prepared machine-ground colours in transportable tubes radically altered the position of the landscape painter: artists could now take to the open air fully equipped and ready to paint just as Renoir and his friends did on their first visit to the forest of Fontainebleau.

This was important in itself, but there were also great advances being made in the type of paints and media, which affected the way artists used their paints from the 1860s onwards. Because linseed oil tended to yellow the paint as it dried, artists had in the past built up the pictures in very thin layers, waiting for each in turn to dry. This was not only a very slow process, but also one that threatened the long-term stability of the picture. Although the yellowing process could be reduced, the complex chemical reactions of the different layers of paint, some thick and some thinner, some closer and some further from the surface, tended to lead to cracking or shrinking as the picture aged. The spontaneity and immediacy of the Impressionists' work was to some extent stimulated by the ready availability of prepared paint, but was also the result of a desire to avoid painting in many layers, thereby minimizing these chemical reactions.

By the mid-nineteenth century poppy-seed oil was beginning to supersede linseed as the favoured binding medium for the machine-ground colours because it tended to yellow less as it dried. A side effect of this was that the paint itself became somewhat stiffer in texture and tended to retain the mark of the brush, something the Impressionists were swift to adopt into their painting vocabulary. Poppy-seed oil also dried rather more slowly, which allowed the artists to work their colours wet into wet on the surface of the canvas without having to mix them laboriously beforehand. Artists who did not like the buttery texture of the prepared paints would often drain them of oil first by putting them on blotting paper, a method Renoir liked because he found that the paint,

PIERRE-AUGUSTE RENOIR
Frédéric Bazille at his Easel
1867
Musée d'Orsay, Paris

This portrait of Bazille at work, like his own portrait of Renoir, was probably painted in Bazille's studio, which both Renoir and Monet shared for a time. The sitter is shown at work on a painting which still exists, *Still Life with Heron*. The actual painting is tight and carefully handled, but Renoir's version shows a broad and free treatment that does not match the fine brush he is using.

once dried of its oil, developed a chalky pastel-like quality which could be used to achieve a feathery softness of touch.

Before a painting could begin, the canvas had to be stretched and primed. Until the mid-nineteenth century it had been the tradition to prime the canvas with a sombre dark brown, but this slowly began to change, and the Impressionist painters nearly always used canvases primed in white or other pale colours. These light grounds tended to give a painting greater luminosity, and also led to the idea of using the colour of the priming as a colour or tonal value in its own right. The ground could be left bare in places to show through, or just covered with a thin layer of paint, blending with or contributing to the other colours on the canvas. Moreover, to contribute further to the speed of execution so important to the Impressionists, the priming tint could be chosen in advance to suit a particular effect of light or weather.

The development of photography could not fail to have an important impact on the nature of painting. Despite much atavistic reluctance to accommodate it, photography began to release painters from the demands of painstaking reproduction, freeing them to explore the problems of painting itself. Photographs also changed the way artists viewed composition: the unselective eye of the camera altered the focus of attention, leading to a flatter overall vision which contrasted with the previously more selective painter's vision. The Impressionist painters were quick to become aware of this, and to realize that a painting need not be a concentrated theatre of action with a central focal point but, like a photograph, could merely be a "slice of life" hinting at action going on outside the immediate frame. This absorption of the lessons of the photograph led to a new type of painting with a more uniform focus, thicker, more even overall paint surfaces, and flattened pictorial perspectives, confusing the more conservative-minded viewers, who failed to grasp the pictorial intentions of this work which no longer seemed to conform to the traditional Beaux Arts standards.

The search for patrons

The development of Impressionism was temporarily halted by the outbreak of the Franco-Prussian war in

PIERRE-AUGUSTE RENOIR
The Pont des Arts, Paris
1867
Norton Simon Foundation, Los Angeles

As a young man Renoir, like his friend Monet, painted urban landscapes, trying to capture the feel of contemporary Paris with its new bridges and boulevards. This work shows signs of the style that he was later to develop into his own version of Impressionism. The influence of photography can also be seen in the wide angle and the way the action is cropped at the edges of the painting.

1870. The group became scattered. Bazille was killed fighting at Beaune la Roland; Monet, Pissarro and Sisley sought refuge in England — the latter was of British descent, and his family had become bankrupt as a result of the war — and Renoir himself joined the Cuirassiers. He saw no action, being posted to the remote town of Pau in the Basses-Pyrénées, but he had little time for painting. On being discharged he returned to Paris, and was one of the few painters to remain there during the troubled period of the Commune.

With his friend and benefactor Bazille now gone, Renoir found life far from easy, but in 1873 a turning point came when the dealer Paul Durand-Ruel began to buy his work, enabling him to rent his first studio, at 35 rue St Georges. He continued to send paintings to the Salon, among them his *Diana*, classical in subject matter and concept but rather more modern in handling. This, like most of his entries, was rejected, and his friends Monet and Pissarro were also in general unsuccessful. Both Monet and Renoir did, in fact, have paintings accepted in 1865 and 1866, but simply being hung in the Salon did not necessarily guarantee success — an unknown artist could find his work placed in a dim corner or so high up on a wall as to render it to all intents and purposes invisible.

The difficulty of gaining acceptance at the Salon, then literally the only showplace for an aspiring artist, led to the idea of staging an independent exhibition where the public could see and judge the young artists' work for themselves. Renoir became treasurer of the newly formed group and served on the hanging committee. The first Impressionist Exhibition was held in 1874, with six paintings by Renoir included. Predictably, the show was a financial disaster, and aroused both hostility and derision from the critics, but of the few works that did sell, several were by Renoir.

The dealer Durand-Ruel had been forced to stop buying, being in financial difficulties, and the group of artists had now no source of income or prospects, so the following year Renoir joined with Monet, Sisley and Berthe Morisot and held an auction sale of their work at the Hôtel Drouot. This once again was a disaster, although Renoir found a patron in the person of a modestly well-to-do customs official, Victor Chocquet, who had come to the auction quite by chance and was one of the few buyers. Chocquet was to become an important patron, not only of Renoir, but also of other avant-garde painters, notably Paul Cézanne.

Throughout the early 1870s Renoir continued to work with Monet, painting on the banks of the Seine and on

RENOIR'S PAINTING METHODS

In this detail from La Grenouillère, *we see how Renoir has worked wet into wet to create the effect of the watery reflection.*

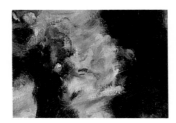

In Box at the Theatre *the thickest paint, unusually, is to be found in the dark areas and in the red of the roses.*

This detail from The Umbrellas *shows Renoir's favourite white ground reflecting back through the thinned paint.*

Renoir's paintings are characterized by a light, feathery and delicate touch (which may owe something to his early training as a porcelain painter) and an obvious delight in the sensual qualities of oil paint. He was always a devoted student of the Old Masters, and his fluid handling of paint owes as much to them as to the Impressionists.

He liked to work on a smooth white or pale-primed canvas, and would often add an extra coating of flake white thinned with oil and turpentine to give extra smoothness. His colours were in general used quite thin, diluted with oil or turpentine, though in places he would build up the paint more thickly, so that each painting shows a considerable variety of paint texture.

He would begin a painting by putting small dabs of thinned colour all over the canvas, apparently at random, but actually to give him an idea of the colour relationships. After this, he would blend them all together, rubbing all over the canvas so that a soft, shadowy image of the whole painting quickly began to appear. He said himself that he would "arrange my subject as I want it, then I start painting as if I were a child. I want a red to sing out like a bell. If it doesn't, I add reds and other colours until I get there." When the lay-in was complete he would begin to define and build up each area, increasing the proportion of oil to turpentine in accordance with the old maxim, "start lean, finish fat."

The colours shown here, with the addition of flake white, are representative of Renoir's palette at the time of this work, Les Grandes Baigneuses. *He always used black (except for a short time during his outdoor painting phase) but, as he said himself, "in mixtures, as in nature."*

1 Naples yellow; 2 Yellow ocher; 3 Raw sienna; 4 Red ocher; 5 Red madder; 6 Terre verte; 7 Veronese (emerald) green; 8 Cobalt blue; 9 Ivory black

the Normandy coast, but as the need for commissions was ever pressing he began to turn increasingly to portraiture. This found him more favour with the buying public, though it was not until Chocquet introduced him to the publisher Georges Charpentier that he really found success. In 1879 his portrait of *Mme Charpentier and her Children* (see page 39) was not only accepted at the Salon but also enjoyed considerable critical acclaim. Renoir had found that the series of Impressionist Exhibitions, which continued until 1886, did not give him the public platform he needed, and although his return to the official Salon was criticized by some of his fellow artists, he stood firm on his decision. As he said to Durand-Ruel, "I would like to tell these gentlemen that I am not going to give up exhibiting at the Salon. This is not for pleasure, but as I told you, it will dispel the revolutionary taint which frightens me...it is a small weakness for which I hope to be pardoned." In fact Renoir was displaying his inherent conservatism both as an individual and as a painter: now beginning to be accepted as a portrait painter of consequence, he was reluctant to jeopardize his precarious success by too-close association with those the public regarded as revolutionaries. But he had aesthetic reasons too, explaining to his friend Ambroise Vollard that, "I have been to the very end of Impressionism and arrived at the conclusion that I knew not how to paint or draw. In a word I was at a dead end."

A change of direction

Although remaining close friends with the Impressionist group and other associated artists such as Cézanne, Renoir was by the end of the decade developing his own style. In 1881 he travelled through Africa — in the footsteps of Delacroix, as he saw it — and then to Italy. In Rome, Florence and Venice, he studied the Italian Renaissance and post-Renaissance masters, which filled him with doubts about the "mainstream" Impressionism practiced by Monet, Pissarro and Sisley. Although some of his paintings, those owned by Durand-Ruel, were put into the seventh Impressionist Exhibition (1882), he was unhappy about exhibiting with Pissarro and the young Gauguin, feeling that they were becoming too unorthodox in their works. As he later said to his young pupil Albert André, "For my part I always defended myself against the charge of being a revolutionary. I always believed and I still believe that I only continued to do what others had done a great deal better before me."

His style became more refined and traditional, and he began to concentrate on the human form to an even greater degree than he had earlier in works such as the *Moulin de la Galette* of 1876 (see page 29). Landscape became almost totally excluded; in *The Umbrellas* (see page 42), for example, the whole space seems to be defined by bodies and umbrellas. This new trend also helped his reputation with the buying public and with Durand-Ruel who, now back on the scene, was at last beginning to secure him a modest income. He began to concentrate much more on the influence of eighteenth-century painters — his old favourites Fragonard and Boucher — as well as on the Neo-classical nineteenth-century figures, Jean-Auguste-Dominique Ingres in particular. His great work of the 1880s, and the final statement of how he had moved away from Impressionism, was *The Bathers* of 1887 (see page 59), for which he made many posed and studied preparatory drawings, in keeping with eighteenth-century tradition. He turned his back on the reliance upon nature which had been so characteristic of his earlier work and continued to be of supreme importance to Monet, Sisley and Pissarro. A remark made to Albert André in his old age seems to confirm his essentially conservative approach. "I discovered about 1883 that the only worthwhile thing for a painter is to study in the museums." Renoir took his study of the Old Masters and eighteenth-century painters very seriously, and by the end of his life he possibly felt that he had learned more of value from them than he had from studying nature and working in the open air with his friends.

Material success and declining health

During this period, family life came to be of increasing importance to Renoir, who was by this time well into his forties. Although he did not marry his mistress Aline Charigot until 1890, she had borne him a son, Pierre, in 1885. At the same time he was also becoming more firmly established with the buying public; a new dealer, Georges Petit, was taking an interest in his work, and in 1886 Durand-Ruel exhibited over thirty paintings in New York (although the *New York Sun* did describe his nudes as "lumpy and obnoxious creatures"). Family life provided a new and stimulating range of subject matter which was to remain a popular theme through the birth of two further sons, Jean in 1894 and Claude (or "Coco") in 1901. His wife's cousin Gabrielle came to live with the family in the 1890s, and became one of Renoir's favourite models as well as a studio assistant, carefully preparing his paint and canvases as he became increasingly infirm.

From the mid-1890s Renoir was dogged by constant ill-health. Bronchial trouble and arthritis prompted a move to the south of France at the turn of the century,

PIERRE-AUGUSTE RENOIR
The Artist's Family
1896
Barnes Foundation, Merion,
Pennsylvania

Here Renoir has depicted his
wife Aline and her two eldest

sons, Pierre and Jean. Claude
was not yet born. The kneeling
girl is Gabrielle, a cousin of
Aline, and a frequent model
for Renoir. The other girl is
not a member of the family;
she is probably a friend or
servant.

and the family bought a house at Cagnes. However, at last
he had no financial problems; his work was becoming
increasingly popular, and he was able to adopt the life-
style of the successful professional middle-class. Dealers
and private collectors alike competed for his work, and
fashionable people sought him out to commission portraits. His enthusiasm for painting never waned, despite
a severe hernia in 1908 and a stroke in 1912 which left
him temporarily paralysed. Gabrielle would arrange for
him to be carried in a sedan chair to his chosen location
in the sunlight or indoors and then prepare the paints on
the palette before inserting the brushes between his stiff
and arthritic fingers. Despite pain and ill-health Renoir
claimed to be very happy in the last years of his life — he
now had nothing to do but paint.

Conclusion

Renoir had always had a sanguine appreciation of his
own worth as a painter and a great respect for his craft,
possibly the result of his working-class background and
apprenticeship as a porcelain painter. He saw himself as
a workman painter with a job to do rather than as an
"artist." Jean Renoir, in his book *Renoir My Father*, lays
great emphasis on the particular manner in which his
father prepared his paints and his canvases. "Renoir used
only eight or ten colours at most. They were ranged in
neat little mounds around the edge of the scrupulously
clean palette. From this modest assortment would come
his shimmering silks and his luminous flesh tones."
Renoir never went in for theorizing about painting,
leaving this to others around him, and according to Jean,
his dislike of such talk once prompted him to complain
of critics, "What is to be done about these literary people
who will never understand that painting is a craft, and
that the material side of it comes first? The ideas come
afterwards when the picture is finished." Although he
had participated in one of the greatest artistic movements in history, it was his essential modesty and conservatism that came to characterize his work.

In 1919, shortly before his death, Renoir was invited to
the Louvre to witness the hanging of his portrait of *Mme
Charpentier*. Arriving in his wheelchair, he was treated
with the greatest respect. After the ceremony he com-
mented, "If I had been presented at the Louvre thirty
years ago in a wheelchair I would have been shown the
door. One has to live a long time to witness such changes.
I have had that chance." In fact Renoir had become a
pillar of respectability, even being made a Chevalier of
the Légion d'Honneur in 1900, and had written to Monet
asking forgiveness for his willingness to pander to the
establishment. It is, however, the key to Renoir's appeal
that his ability to make changes led him to combine
many of his Impressionist techniques with a more
formal sense of pictorial subject matter and style derived
from the traditions of the eighteenth-century, producing
a style uniquely suited to him and much admired to this
day. It is also a tribute to his warm and open personality
that, in spite of turning away from Impressionism, he
nevertheless retained the affection of his fellow painters,
and that he contrived a peaceful, successful and satis-
fying life in spite of his early tribulations.

CHRONOLOGY OF RENOIR'S LIFE

1841   25 February: born in Limoges, sixth child of Léonard Renoir and Marguerite Merlot.

1844   Family moves to Paris.

1856   Becomes apprentice porcelain painter to Lévy frères.

1862   Enters studio of Charles Gleyre and meets Monet, Sisley and Bazille.

1863   Meets Courbet and Pissarro.

1866   Lise Trehot becomes his model and mistress.

1869   Frequents Café Guerbois and meets Degas, Manet and Zola.

1868   Paints *La Grenouillère*.

1870-71   Franco-Prussian War and Paris Commune.

1872   Introduced by Monet to Paul Durand-Ruel.

1874   First Impressionist Exhibition. Paints *Box at the Theatre* and *The Dancer*.

1875   Meets Victor Chocquet and Georges Charpentier.

1876   Second Impressionist Exhibition. Paints *The Ball at the Moulin de la Galette* and *The Swing*.

1878   Paints *Mme Charpentier and her Children*.

1879   Enjoys first critical success at the Salon with *Mme Charpentier*. Meets future wife, Aline Charigot.

1881   Begins *The Umbrellas*.

1881-82   Travels in North Africa and Italy.

The Box at the Theater

The Umbrellas

Girls at the Piano

1883   First exhibition of paintings in the US.

1885   Aline gives birth to first son, Pierre.

1887   Paints *The Bathers*.

1888   First attack of rheumatoid arthritis.

1890   Marries Aline.

1892   Paints *Girls at the Piano*, which becomes the first purchase of his work by the French state.

1894   Birth of second son, Jean. Death of Gustave Caillebotte; Renoir appointed executor.

1897   Caillebotte bequests partially accepted by French state.

1898   Buys house in Essoyes in South of France.

1900   Appointed Chevalier of the Légion d'Honneur.

1901   Birth of third son, Claude ("Coco").

1906   Paints portrait of Misia Natanson.

1907   Buys house, "Les Collettes," in Cagnes and has a special studio built.

1912   Suffers a stroke but recovers.

1914-18   First World War. Sons Pierre and Jean wounded. Aline dies (1915).

1918   Begins *Les Grandes Baigneuses*.

1919   Made Commander of the Légion d'Honneur.

1919   December 3: dies and is buried next to Aline in Essoyes.

THE PAINTINGS

LA GRENOUILLERE

1868
26×37in/66×94cm
Oil on canvas
National Museum, Stockholm

A contemporary description of the riverside resort of La Grenouillère in *L'Evénement l'Illustré*, June, 1868, describes it thus: "Trouville on the banks of the Seine: a meeting place for the noisy well-dressed crowds that emigrate from Paris and set up camp in Croissy, Chatou or Bougival for the summer...on a well-tarred old barge firmly moored to the bank...stands a wooden hut." The pictures that Renoir painted here are perhaps the most Impressionist of his whole *oeuvre*, indeed it was here that he and his friend Monet, painting side by side in the summer of 1868, developed the new ideas about painting that had been growing in them throughout the decade. Monet wrote to Bazille a few weeks before they began work, "I have a dream, a painting, the baths of La Grenouillère for which I have done a few bad sketches, but it is a dream. Renoir, who has just spent two months here, also wants to do this painting." Each executed three different versions of the scene, casual moments in the life of the resort caught with swift and sudden strokes of the brush to give a strong sense of immediacy — a few minutes caught before the light changed or the party broke up.

For such outdoor work Renoir used some special equipment: a folding easel, wooden palette, travelling paintbox and ready prepared canvases on stretchers. These were not primed with the traditional dark brown ground used by his predecessors, but with a white or warm, pale ground which helped to enhance the luminosity of the painting. This work would have been done very swiftly, certainly in a day and possibly even less. The rapid brushstrokes are large in the foreground and smaller in the distance, giving a feeling of depth to the scene. Light grounds make it more difficult to create depth, but it

was not long before the Impressionists came to appreciate and cultivate that sense of flatness because they were more interested in the picture surface than in traditional perspective. As can be seen here, Renoir has deliberately blurred detail, dissolved clear lines and avoided giving solidity to his figures, thus encouraging the viewer to participate in the painting and interpret it for himself. He has used variations in the size and intensity of the brushstrokes to express form, so that the figures are not so much drawn as created by the merging of colours and brushstrokes.

The thicker paint resulting from mixing with poppy-seed oil rather than linseed oil stands up on the canvas instead of sinking into it, enabling Renoir to work wet into wet, as in the red boat in the middle distance. Short horizontal strokes have been used to indicate the light shimmering on the water, while wavy vertical strokes describe the reflections of the foreground boats. The brushwork is an important part of the painting, and he has made no attempt to achieve the kind of smooth finish which more academic painters strove for. The palette is fairly muted, with browns, greens and blues set off in places with reds, but more generally just highlighted in white. It is interesting to compare this work with Monet's version (opposite). Renoir has placed greater emphasis on figures, while in Monet's painting they have been allowed to recede into the distance and become absorbed into the landscape. Also, Monet's chief preoccupation has been with the shimmering water, which seems almost to dominate his work. Each artist has expressed his own feelings and rendered his own particular and intimate vision, but neither was attempting objectivity — the uniqueness of approach was of paramount importance.

La Grenouillère was a fashionable place for eating, swimming and boating on the outskirts of Paris — now absorbed into the suburbs. In the summer of 1868 Renoir and Monet each painted several versions of the place from different viewpoints. As can be seen from a comparison of the two paintings, each had his own particular vision, but both were concerned with capturing an immediate moment in swift, bold brush-strokes. This picture, painted directly onto the canvas with no preliminary drawing, would have been completed in a matter of hours in order to be finished before the light changed.

CLAUDE MONET
La Grenouillère
1869
Metropolitan Museum, New York

Monet and Renoir painted together at La Grenouillère (the name of which literally means "the frog-pond"), placing their easels side by side, but comparison of the two paintings clearly shows their different preoccupations. Monet was most interested in the effects of water; the figures have been pushed away from the foreground and play a less prominent role than in Renoir's painting of the same scene.

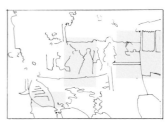

1 Swift, firm brushstrokes have been used to create the figures and the boats, which merge almost indistinguishably into the water, with the reflections and the objects reflected becoming blurred in blobs of vivid colour. The poster on the side of the barge and the tablecloth hanging over the edge are painted loosely, hints rather than literal descriptions.

2 Larger strokes of the brush have been used in the foreground, and the water is built up with a series of horizontal strokes which contrast with the vertical of the boat's stern.

3 *Actual size detail* In contrast with Monet's painting (see previous page) the figures play a dominant role, but they are still very loosely painted. In a rapidly executed work such as this, the paints are applied over and beside one another while still wet, so that they blend into and modify each other. This is particularly noticeable in the stripes of the man's trousers.

1

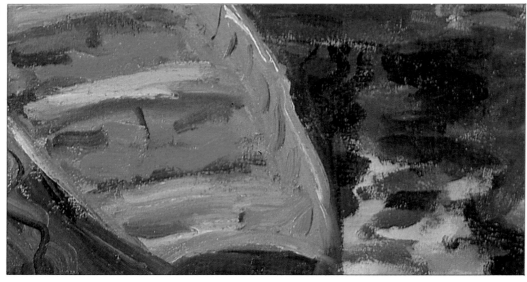

2

3 Actual size detail

THE BOX AT THE THEATRE

(La Loge)
1874
31½×25in/80×63.5cm
Oil on canvas
Courtauld Institute Galleries, London

The models for this work were Renoir's brother Edmond and one of his favourite female models, Nini, nicknamed "La Geule de Raie" ("fish-mouth"). The setting is a theatre box, with two elegant Parisians dressed in their finery at an evening gathering — the theatre was a place both to see and be seen. The choice of subject reflects the modern trend in painting: Charles Baudelaire, writing in the middle of the century, had argued for a painter of contemporary life who would forget the heroes of old and depict modern man in his top hat and tails, the embodiment of the new France. But in this work Renoir has moved a long way from the Impressionist style of *La Grenouillère* (see page 17) to a deliberately posed and constructed work. Here we see, not the immediacy of the fleeting moment swiftly placed on canvas, but a well-constructed and thought-out scene of intimacy as we spy on the young couple watching the play before them. Despite this, the work is very modern in its handling and composition, and the way the front of the box cuts diagonally through the foreground and the face of the man is hidden from the viewer by his opera glasses is distinctly unconventional.

The painting was exhibited at the first Impressionist Exhibition in 1874, and despite the scorn aroused by the exhibition it was one of the few pictures to find a buyer. It was sold to the dealer Père Martin for 450 francs, quite a small price in comparison to the 1000 francs or so that Pissarro could command for a landscape.

Although Renoir was now beginning to move away from the outdoor landscapes with which Monet was still preoccupied, he seemed to bring to his indoor settings much of the knowledge and understanding of sunlight and shadow gained from his work in the open air. There is still an overall warmth, the result of the light-coloured priming he used — and the shadows are full of reflected light and colour. Instead of a dark background, the figures in their evening clothes are set against a light brown, which emphasizes the fact that he has used black as a colour in itself rather than just as a tone for the shadows. The paint surface is quite unlike that in *La Grenouillère*, much thinner, and with none of the thick textural impastos of the earlier painting, and it has been worked into a far smoother finish. Renoir made the paints more "juicy" by thinning them with turpentine and working into them while still wet so that they have mixed into each other on the canvas, marvellously creating the effect of the blues and violets of the shadows reflecting back onto the whites of the man's shirt front and woman's lace. The warm ground shows through the thin paint, enhancing the translucence of the painting and giving more body to the applied paint, as in the woman's forearms. This technique also helps to avoid the use of too many layers of paint and excessive re-working of the surface. Where shadows are required in the folds of the dress or the shirt, more local colour has been used mixed with the white, helping to define the contours and give the forms structure. The technique differs from the traditional one used by the Old Masters, which involved building up from dark to light, in that the thinnest paint is to be found in the highlights and white areas and the thickest in the dark areas of the clothes and the red of the roses. The black comes entirely into its own and takes on a majestic quality in contrast to the gold and the pink.

Renoir seems to have taken to heart the writer Charles Baudelaire's plea for a painter of modern life, and here we see two elegant Parisians, in all their finery, on display at the theater. But it is not the subject matter alone that betrays the modernity of the painting; the composition is equally unconventional, with the bold diagonal across the front of the painting, and the man's face obscured by his opera glasses. Renoir has here used black as a colour in its own right, contrasting the clothing against the pale background that was to become a typical feature of Impressionist works.

1

1 The unusual compositional device of obscuring the man's face adds particular interest to this work. The shadows beneath the opera glasses have taken on a black hue, and the flesh tones of the face have also absorbed some of the surrounding colouration.

2 Whites and blacks are seldom seen pure in nature, as they reflect and absorb the local light. Here the white gloves have taken on blue hues, giving the hand a greater solidity of form. The gold opera glasses, which provide a diagonal contrast to the man's black ones, have been highlighted with small dashes of white reflected from the dress.

3 *Actual size detail* The central bouquet is very loosely constructed, with just the vaguest of brush-strokes that only register as meaningful definitions of form when viewed from a distance. The white of the bodice is considerably altered in tone by the surrounding blacks, and the small touches of red and gold add interest to what is essentially a monochromatic central focus of blacks and whites in various shades.

2

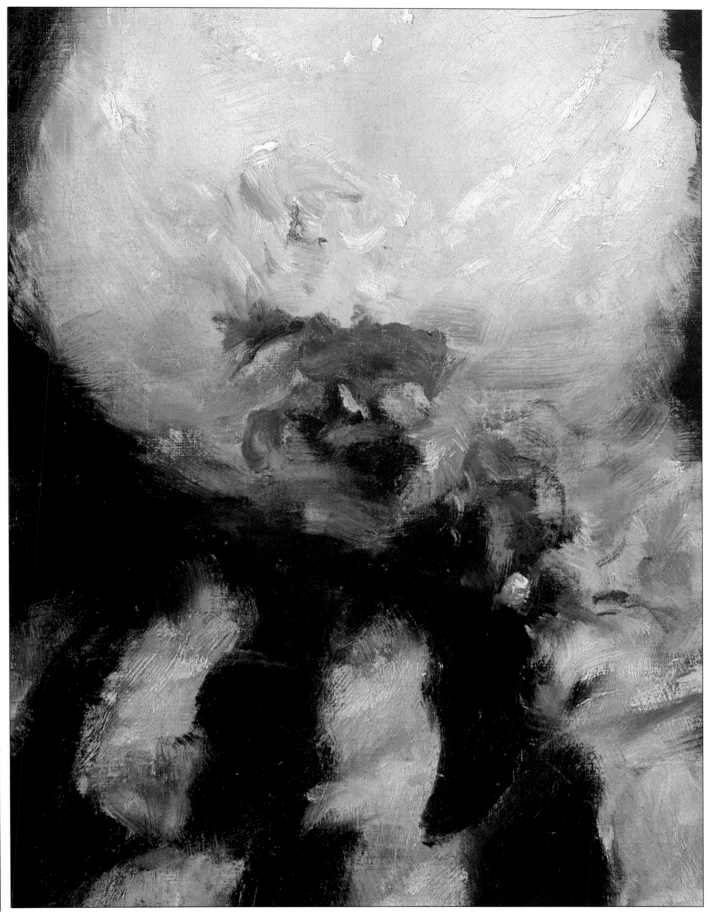

3 *Actual size detail*

The Dancer

(La Danseuse)

1874

$56\frac{1}{8} \times 37\frac{1}{8}$ in / 142.5×94 cm

Oil on canvas

National Gallery of Art, Washington

The critic Louis Leroy, whose mockery of Monet's work *Impression, Sunrise* at the first Impressionist Exhibition in 1874 unwittingly coined the word "impressionist," had only one comment to make about this offering of Renoir's in the same exhibition. He singled out *The Dancer* as an example of Renoir's lack of form and depth, complaining that "his dancer's legs are as cottony as the gauze of her skirt." But Leroy's damning opinions did not deter the dealer Durand-Ruel, who bought the painting, sold it two years later for 1000 francs to Charles Deudon, a wealthy clothing manufacturer, and bought it back again for considerably more in the 1890s.

In fact this lovely painting marvellously exhibits Renoir's talent and the subtlety of his technique. It differs greatly in both method and presentation from *The Box at the Theatre* (see page 21), painted in the same year. The composition is straightforward and direct, and seems to have been influenced by Manet's work of the 1860s, *The Fife-player*. Like Manet, Renoir has used a full-face light falling evenly and directly on the model, but with less of the harshness and strong tonal contrast of Manet, so that the outlines become softer and more diffused. The figure is indistinctly located, with an absence of floor or wall angles to define the room, and only a minimal shadow cast by the dancer herself. Degas' influence can also be seen in this work, but although using the same subject, Renoir has taken a very different approach. This is not a dancer appearing on stage, nor one practising exercises or lacing her shoes preparatory to dancing, but one who, having danced and left the stage, is once again ready to resume her character as an ordinary person.

Renoir has used a very restrained palette here; the small touches of pink and blue seem almost to leap out from the subdued tones of the dress, which itself merges gently into the background. Once again a pale ground has been used to give a sense of warmth and lightness, and this can be seen showing through the paint, which has been applied very thinly by mixing with turpentine on the palette. Only the most delicate of highlights have been used on the pink shoes, the ribbons and the handkerchief, which helps to emphasize the lack of recession in the painting and give a feeling of intimacy which a formal staged setting would have lost. The blue of the waistband is echoed in the frilly gauze of the dress. This does indeed have the "cottony" texture remarked on by Leroy, but despite the softness of the work the figure does not lack solidity, which has been achieved by the minimal use of shadows around the feet and legs.

The model for this work was Ninette Legrand, the sister of Alphonse Legrand, who had worked for Durand-Ruel, but in 1874 had established a gallery of his own. Legrand was a close friend of Renoir and tried by auctions and other means to interest the buying public in his work. In 1877 he became the agent for Maclean's, a London-based cement company. Renoir, who had conceived the idea of executing large-scale murals, experimented on Maclean cement, which contained a fine white plaster that gave the works considerably heightened luminosity. This may well have influenced the increasingly smooth white grounds which he began to use as canvas priming in the 1880s.

This painting shows the influence of the more figurative side of Impressionism as practised by Manet and Degas, both of whom were associated with, but not strictly part of, the movement. The composition owes a debt to Manet's painting *The Fife-Player* and the choice of subject matter to Degas, though Renoir's treatment is quite different to Degas', the lines being much softer and the paint handling typically light and feathery. The palette itself is restrained, but the painting is nevertheless full of light and warmth. Like *The Box at the Theatre*, this painting was one of those exhibited at the infamous first Impressionist Exhibition held at the studio of the photographer Nadar, and it was bought by the dealer Durand-Ruel.

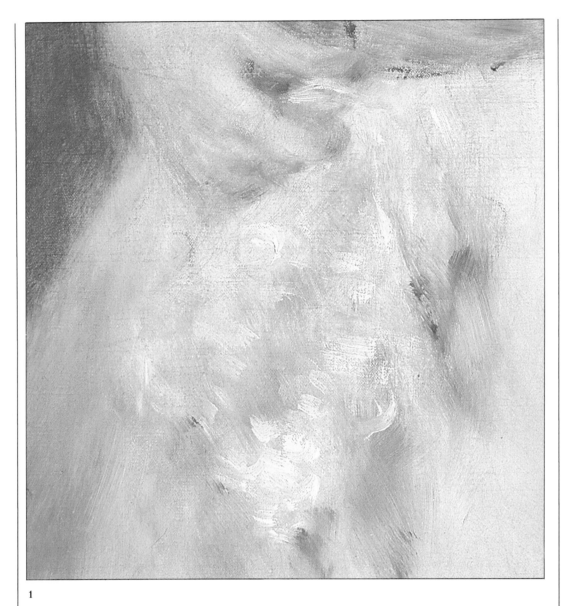

1

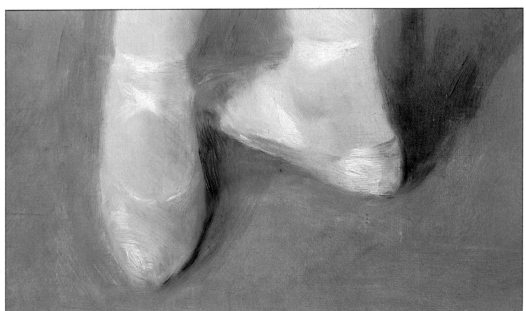

2

1 When looked at from a close viewpoint, as here, the ring of the bouquet shows scarcely any modelling and looks almost insubstantial, but on standing back from the painting one can see the contrast between the short, firm strokes of white and the slightly bluer hues of the skirt. This gives exactly the impression Renoir wanted — one that is destroyed by close examination.

2 The strokes of white have been worked into the pink of the shoes while still wet, enhancing the soft modelling and structure of the slippered feet. The shadow around the feet has been kept to a minimum, but there is just enough to give the figure a sense of solidity against the shadowy, empty background.

3 *Actual size detail* The dancer's head has been more firmly modeled than anything else in the painting other than the shoes. Using soft, feathery strokes of thin paint, Renoir has built up the hair and face so gently that the marks of the brush are almost indiscernible, while in the eyebrows and the ribbon the paint is thicker and the brushwork more noticeable.

3 *Actual size detail*

BALL AT THE MOULIN DE LA GALETTE

1876

51½×69in/130.75×175.25cm

Oil on canvas

Musée d'Orsay, Paris

This painting, Renoir's most ambitious Impressionist genre work, was the fulfilment of an idea that had been maturing for several years. The Moulin de la Galette was a dance hall in a converted mill on the top of Montmartre (then a village on the outskirts of Paris) which specialized in "galettes," sweet thin wafers. It had a large shaded garden, a covered dancing area and a small bandstand. In order to paint the picture Renoir rented a studio in the nearby rue Cortot and went every day to the Moulin to draw and study his subject. His brother Edmond described the process. "How does he go about painting Le Moulin de la Galette? He goes to live there for six months, makes friends with all that little world that has its own style, which models copying their poses would not render, and in the midst of the whirl of the popular merry-go-round he expresses wild movements with a dazzling verve." In fact Renoir painted several sketches in oil and one finished smaller-scale version (now in the collection of Mrs John Hay Whitney of New York) which was carried to and from the Moulin every day by Renoir and his friends. Many of these friends are featured in the painting: dancing with the figure in pink, Marguerite Legrand, is the painter Don Pedro Vidal de Solares y Cardeñas, and around the table to the right are seated Franc Lamy, Norbert Goeneutte and Georges Rivière. The final version was painted in the garden of the rue Cortot studio as the canvas was too large to move, and his friends came there to pose for him.

This is a very sophisticated and complex painting showing an impressive grasp of depth and perspective. The preparatory ground is a warm pink, contributing to the overall tone, although here it is not left to show through the paint. Renoir's chief concern, and the one that gives the painting much of its pictorial interest and charm, is the effect of dappled sunlight on the moving figures. This has been achieved by scumbling, mixing colours on the surface of the canvas while still wet, and by introducing occasional white highlights into the wet paint of the clothes and hats. Unlike in some earlier works, for example *The Box at the Theatre* (see page 21), the highlights and brighter areas of the picture are actually loaded with thicker paint, and the whole texture of the surface is much thicker than in *The Dancer* (see page 25). The vigorous brushstrokes help to convey a sense of movement and excitement in the figures, and the light seems almost to be moving on the surface of the canvas as it flits over the dancers.

The painting was exhibited at the third Impressionist Exhibition in 1877, and was afterwards acquired by Renoir's friend and fellow-painter Gustave Caillebotte, who bequeathed it to the French nation on his death in 1894. Georges Rivière, a critic and one of the sitters for the painting, wrote an appreciation of it in his review of the exhibition which probably expressed to some extent Renoir's own feelings about the work. "In a garden inundated with sunlight, barely shaded by some spindly acacia plants whose foliage trembles with the least breeze, there are charming young girls in all the freshness of their fifteen years, proud of their light homemade dresses fashioned of inexpensive material, and young men full of gaiety...noise, laughter, movement, sunshine in an atmosphere of youth. Such is 'Le Bal au Moulin de la Galette' by Renoir."

This is Renoir's most
ambitious Impressionist genre
painting. It is a sophisticated,
complex work combining
tremendous movement and
excitement with the
wonderful effect of broken
sunlight filtered through the
overhanging trees and
dappling the figures as they
dance or sit talking at the
tables. The proceeds of a
portrait commission had
enabled Renoir to rent a studio
in Montmartre, near the dance
hall, and he worked on the
preliminary oil-sketch for the
painting for several months,
carrying the canvas from the
studio to the Moulin so that he
could paint on the spot and
lose nothing of the immediacy
of the scene. The final, full-
scale version was painted in
the garden of the studio,
where his friends came to
pose for him, as the canvas
was too large to be moved

1 The dancing couple in the middle distance have been painted with long, swift strokes that create a strong sense of movement. The woman's arms have been quite loosely executed, and on her dress, the colours have blurred into one another, with blue mixing into the white, evoking the feel of the rapid, whirling dance.

2 This detail is a marvellous study of dappled sunlight, full of colour, not only in the man's yellow boater with its touches of blue, yellow, red and white, but also in the head of the small boy. This, framed by objects on various different pictorial planes, seems to glow out at us, and even the woman's blue dress in the shade of the trees reflects a spectrum of other colours.

1

2

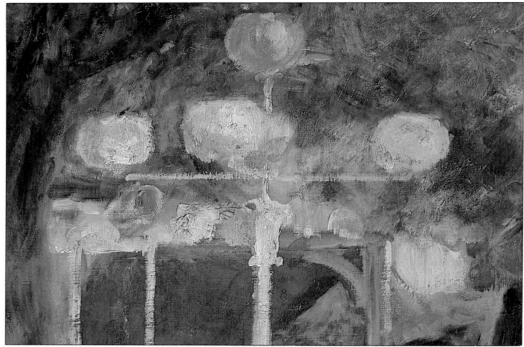

3

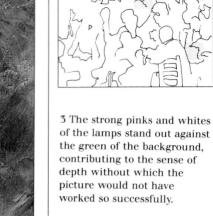

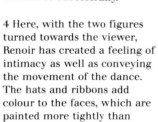

3 The strong pinks and whites of the lamps stand out against the green of the background, contributing to the sense of depth without which the picture would not have worked so successfully.

4 Here, with the two figures turned towards the viewer, Renoir has created a feeling of intimacy as well as conveying the movement of the dance. The hats and ribbons add colour to the faces, which are painted more tightly than their surroundings.

5 *Actual size detail* The glasses on the table have absorbed all the colour of their surroundings, but Renoir has nevertheless given them definition, achieved by the use of small highlights in white. Because the paint has been applied wet into wet, however, even these highlights have taken on some of the surrounding blue, so that they are subtle and delicate.

4

5 Actual size detail

THE SWING

(La Balançoire)
1876
36¼ × 28¾ in / 92 × 73 cm
Oil on canvas
Musée d'Orsay, Paris

This work was produced while Renoir was painting *Ball at the Moulin de la Galette* (see page 29) in the garden of his studio in the rue Cortot. The theme is derived from a lovely, delicate work by Fragonard, although the handling is entirely modern and fresh. The models are Marguerite Legrand, who can be seen dancing in the other painting, and once again his brother Edmond with the painter Norbert Goeneutte. This picture was also bought by the painter Gustave Caillebotte and formed part of the controversial Caillebotte bequest in 1894. Renoir, an old friend of Caillebotte, was made an executor of his will, and it was only after considerable time and trouble that the majority — but by no means all — of the bequest was accepted by the nation and hung in the Luxembourg Palace.

After the tightly constructed composition of the *Ball at the Moulin de la Galette*, *The Swing* comes as a refreshingly intimate work. The off-white priming pushes forward through the paint to throw the colour-enriched light back towards the viewer, and where the ground itself shows through its colour has been actively exploited among the applied colours to reduce the need for excessive working of the surface. The paint, however, is much thicker than was usual for Renoir at the time. The brightness of the colours is markedly dependent on the relationship of each one with the adjoining colours, so that the white of the dress actually takes on many of the blues and purples of the shadows behind, and the coat of the foreground man serves to unite the painting in a luminous whole.

The freshness of the work is to some extent the result of the absence of any strong lines. Renoir seems in this instance to have heeded the advice of Cézanne, who observed that "drawing and colour are not separate at all; insofar as you paint you draw. The more colour harmonizes the more exact the drawing becomes." It is the careful use of colours that defines the shape and mass of all the figures, and it is blue above all other colours that Renoir has used most effectively in this picture. Jean Renoir in *Renoir My Father* remarked on the importance of blue in the construction of the paintings. "I now come back to the question of his theories...he would indicate his shadows with cobalt blue, and this blue shadow would determine the position of the whole picture, and even the subject. He would select this or that spot because the shadow was blue there; and it is the cobalt blue, and not the original inspiration of the work, that creates the message we get from the picture."

The construction of *The Swing*, although not disciplined in the way of the *Moulin de la Galette* is, is nevertheless very deliberate. The focal point is the woman in white, swinging lightly in the warm haze of a summer afternoon, and the eye is drawn to her not only by the use of colour but also by the deliberate contrast of brushwork. The left of the picture and the background are painted with much looser and longer strokes, which gradually give way to a tighter but flatter surface where the paint is thinner. In the figure of the woman herself the paint is built up considerably thicker and with more impasto, particularly on the highlights of the dress, which stands out against the surrounding blues and violets but at the same time echoes their colours and blends into them.

The theme of this painting was derived from a work of the same title by Fragonard, the eighteenth-century artist whom Renoir had admired since his early days studying in the Louvre. It was painted at the same time as the *Moulin de la Galette* (see page 29), in Renoir's temporary studio in Montmarte, but is a much more intimate work, concentrating on the conversation between the young woman and the two men, observed by a modern "cherub" on the extreme left. There are strong similarities between the two works, however, in the colour and effects of dappled sunlight, and the overall effect of this painting also is created by the use of blue in the shadows, unifying the whole colour scheme, a favorite device of the Impressionists.

1

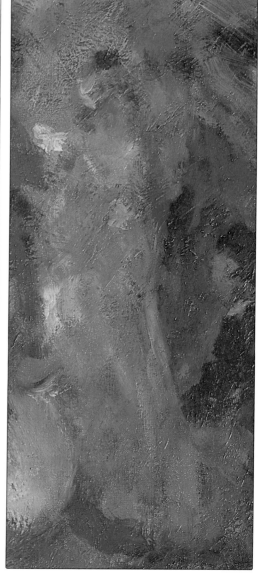

2

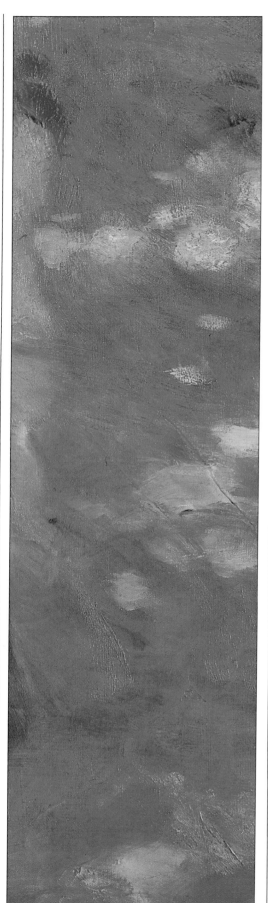

3

1 This detail, of the hand emerging from the sleeve to clutch the swing-rope, shows several of the techniques which were important to Renoir's personal brand of Impressionism. The inside of the sleeve has caught the bluish line of the man's jacket, and the almost formless blob of white on the upper side of the wrist is a description of the brief flash of sunlight from a gap in the leaves above.

2 The two figures behind the girl have been treated very broadly and sketchily so that, although clearly recognizable as a man and a woman, they recede unobtrusively into the background. The colours echo those in the foreground, but in muted form; the red of the flower in the man's buttonhole, for example, is relatively cool.

3 Renoir has used his brush-strokes extremely inventively to create the effect of the sunlight falling on the ground through leaves which are being gently blown by the wind. Some are vertical, some horizontal, and others diagonal, while the colours themselves either blend softly into one another or sit one on top of another in a curious patchwork effect.

4 *Actual size detail* The young woman's expression as she turns half-smiling away from her admirers has been depicted with great feeling and delicacy. Renoir has used short brush-strokes to define the features, creating subtle shadows and just a hint of colour to delineate the mouth and eyebrows.

4 *Actual size detail*

MME CHARPENTIER AND HER CHILDREN

1878
60½ × 74⅞ in / 153.75 × 190 cm
Oil on canvas
Metropolitan Musem of Art, New York

The Charpentier commission was an important moment in Renoir's career. Through an early patron, Victor Chocquet, he had met the publisher Georges Charpentier, who commissioned him to paint his wife and two children, Georgette and Paul. Before he began the painting Renoir decided that he would make it the spearhead of his renewed attempts to find success at the Salon, and he knew that the subject gave him a good chance. As he observed in an interview with the journalist Moncade in 1904, "Mme Charpentier wanted to be in a good position and Mme Charpentier knew the members of the jury whom she lobbied vigorously."

For six weeks Renoir went to the Charpentier town-house in rue de Grenelles and, as Edmond Renoir recalls, "painted her at home, without any of the furniture having been moved from where it stood every day, without anything having been prepared to improve one part of the painting or another...is he doing a portrait? He will ask his model to maintain her customary manner, to sit the way she sits, to dress the way she dresses, so that nothing smacks of discomfort and preparation. That is why in addition to its artistic value, his work has all the 'sui generis' charm of a painting faithful to modern life." Renoir was determined not to be rebuffed again by the critics, and took great care to paint a work which conformed to some of the accepted standards, avoiding the excesses of which he had been accused in the past. The surface of the painting is more alert and clear than in *The Swing* (see page 35), and the brushstrokes are less obvious, so that they do not distract the eye from the essential composition. This is centrally placed and formally constructed in a large triangle with the mother's hand at the apex, so that the viewer's eye moves logically through the faces of the children upward to the mother. In this painting, unlike earlier works, the clothes and objects do not reflect the local colour of their surroundings or adjacent objects, but are clearly defined in themselves, each with its own colour, and each figure is a separate, solid and tangible entity. Renoir has given a chalky, pastel quality to his paint by draining it of some of the oil, which gives the brushwork a feathery delicacy entirely appropriate to the fashionable "Japanese" drawing room of a society lady.

Renoir has not, however, forsaken all his new or progressive techniques in the search for respectability. The colours are vibrant and full of all the excitement one could expect from an Impressionist palette; the setting is thoroughly modern, but above all, the perspective is very daring. The subject is viewed from above, which tends to flatten the perceived picture surface and reduce the sense of depth, bringing the figures forward to the viewer rather than drawing the eye of the viewer into the picture to the subject.

As might have been predicted, the painting had a great success at the Salon. Some of Renoir's painter friends felt betrayed by his efforts to win recognition from the "art establishment," but the pragmatic Pissarro rejoiced in his colleague's good fortune. He wrote to the restaurateur Murer that "Renoir...is having a great success at the Salon. I think he is launched, so much the better, poverty is so hard." And indeed, Renoir was to some extent launched. Commissions now came in fairly regularly, and through the patronage of Mme Charpentier he gradually became able to move into the circle of the *haute bourgeoisie*, where commissions could bring him a comfortable living.

This group portrait of the wife and children of the publisher Georges Charpentier was Renoir's first major commission. It also afforded him his first genuine success at the Salon, since the social standing of the Charpentiers ensured that it was hung where it would gain maximum attention. He tailored some of his more modern techniques to conform to bourgeois taste, and one can see a considerable difference in style and paint handling between this and works such as *The Swing*. The composition is built on the traditional triangle, and each area of colour is clearly defined, with none of the wet-into-wet mixing of colours on the canvas that had characterized his earlier work.

1

2

1 This detail shows a strong contrast of brushwork between the carefully modelled and quite thinly painted faces of the children and the rich, almost scribbled strokes indicating the riot of colour on the patterned sofa back. The left-hand side of this has caught the light, and the colours are rich and vibrant, while the area not in direct light is more soberly treated.

2 Modelling the form of the body underneath the black dress, and at the same time giving the impression of the silk fabric, required brushwork of the highest quality. The folds of the dress catch the light as they follow the contours of the sitter's knees, but this has been achieved, not by applying white on top of the black, but by allowing the white ground underneath the black to show through. The black paint has been used more thinly in the areas where Renoir wanted to create the shimmer of the light-struck fabric.

3 *Actual size detail* In the background of this formally constructed work, Renoir has given us a still life of great beauty, painted much more loosely and fluidly than the figures themselves. With swift, bold strokes of a paint-laden brush, he has run one colour into another, the pink flowers carrying their hues into the white. The blue pattern of the jug has become absorbed into the very form of the jug, and the thickly painted grapes glow in the reflected warmth of the flowers.

3 *Actual size detail*

THE UMBRELLAS

(Les Parapluies)
1881 and 1885
71×45in/180.25×114.25cm
Oil on canvas
National Gallery, London

The Umbrellas has become for English audiences one of the most familiar and best loved of all Renoir's works, since it entered the National Gallery collection as a result of the Lane Bequest in 1917. It is also one of Renoir's most modern paintings in structural terms, and reveals a great deal about his changing styles between the beginning and middle of the 1880s.

The picture was begun in 1881 but not completed until four years later, and it seems likely that it is the result of two separate periods rather than four years of continuous work. The right-hand foreground side of the painting — which includes the girl with a hoop, the other girl half-turned away to her right and the two women beyond — is the earlier. The later part is the left-hand side and background, including the foreground woman with a basket, the man behind her and all the umbrellas through to the top of the painting. These two separate periods add great interest to a work that is in any case full of pictorial complexity. The bold construction is as modern a one as Renoir ever attempted: there is little sense of the figures actually being set in a landscape, as only the very slightest hint has been given of foreground or background. The subject is viewed from above so that the figures are almost tipped to the front of the painting, and the jostle of umbrellas with the many faces beneath further distorts the traditional perspective.

The date of the first period of painting can be arrived at both by comparison with other works of similar handling of the same date and by looking at the women's dresses. Those on the right display the latest fashions of 1881, and the brushwork has the soft, feathery quality which marks Renoir's work before his trip to Italy in 1882 and which gives a certain insubstantiality to the contours and the modelling. The colours are full, fresh and varied, and have been mixed wet into wet on the surface of the canvas. The left-hand and upper part of the painting could not provide a greater contrast. The dress of the woman with the basket — the model for whom was his future wife Aline — is of quite a different cut and much more severe in its lines, a fashion which only came in in 1885 and would have passed out again by 1887. The handling is also different, with the figures much more precisely drawn and the modelling and colours clearer and firmer. Renoir's usual white-primed canvas has been used, which accounts for the luminosity of the light colours coming out through the blue on the right, but on the left, the paint has been applied drier and with greater solidity, which does not allow for the same luminosity. The umbrellas have also been worked more solidly, giving the group on the right the effect of being surrounded in a small bright corner of their own.

Renoir did not enjoy great success with the painting. Durand-Ruel took it into his gallery in 1890 but did not actually buy it until 1892, and it was only acquired by Sir Hugh Lane in 1907. The cause of dissatisfaction was probably the unhappy marriage of two recent women's fashions which, set against each other in such a tightly constructed composition, must have appeared incongruous to contemporaries familiar with the styles of the day. To us, a hundred years later, this is unimportant, and although we can see the sharp contrasts in painting style that characterize the work, we can also appreciate its complex and stimulating construction.

This painting is particularly interesting because Renoir worked on it in two distinct periods, giving us an insight into his changing style at the time. The right-hand side was painted in 1881, and shows the light, feathery brushwork of the previous decade, while the left side was completed four years later. Here the paint has been used much more solidly so that it completely covers the light ground, a technique he began to favour after his long trip to Italy had caused him to doubt the basic tenets of Impressionism.

1

1 Renoir's favourite white priming has been allowed to show through the blue in places to describe the surface of the umbrellas. The faces beneath the umbrellas have been painted tightly in contrast to the broad, loose treatment of the sky and trees, whose very sketchiness serve to emphasize the tighter technique of the later parts of the painting — the left and upper sections.

2 In the right-hand part of the painting, done earlier than the left, Renoir is still using the loosely applied, soft, feathery brush-strokes that characterize his work of the 1870s. Blue appears strongly in the shadows, setting off the warm and luxurious colours, another feature of Renoir's earlier work which ceased in his later paintings.

3 *Actual size detail* The bouquet has been created with short, wide brush-strokes that when seen at a distance combine to give the sense of wholeness Renoir sought. By the subtle use of light on the hand and thumb he has given a complete sense of the form and roundness of the flesh beneath the glove.

2

3 *Actual size detail*

THE BATHERS

(Les Baigneuses)
1887
$46\frac{1}{2} \times 67\frac{1}{4}$in/$118.25 \times 170.75$cm
Oil on canvas
Philadelphia Museum of Art

This painting, Renoir's most ambitious work of the 1880s and the one by which he set greatest store, was executed for an exhibition of his works being prepared by the dealer Georges Petit. Petit had a reputation for providing for the somewhat limited and traditional tastes of the bourgeoisie, and Renoir was conscious of the concessions he might have to make.

The Bathers was meticulously worked on and prepared. There are still over twenty preparatory drawings which show the long struggle that Renoir had with the form and posture of his nudes. Even the foreground, the trees and the drapery were worked on in advance, for Renoir was determined not only to make his name with the public but also to show that his new creed of "irregularity" was appropriate to the execution of a great painting. He had tried to explain this creed to Durand-Ruel in a letter of 1884: the idea was an attempt at escape from symmetry and unity in both architecture and painting, although he was in favour of clear lines, a structured composition and realistic details derived from nature. The adoption of these standards did not preclude the use of loose brushwork or the bright colours and light of Impressionism.

Another important influence on *The Bathers* was the classical treatment of the nude. Since his travels in Italy, where he had seen the monumental frescoes of Michelangelo and Raphael, Renoir had been determined to produce a major work glorifying the female nude in a manner that could rank with the Old Masters. The work of Ingres, too, has a bearing on this painting, for he had contorted the bodies of his nudes in an attempt to emphasize decorative qualities over representational accuracy (though he himself denied that he did anything other than copy nature). Renoir was similarly ambivalent on this subject. "How hard it is to find exactly the point at which imitation of nature must cease in a picture. The painting must not be too close to the model and yet we must be conscious of nature."

In order to achieve some of the effects of fresco Renoir painted *The Bathers* on a specially prepared white-lead oil ground, which gave a very smooth surface. Onto this he first painted the figures with their silky-soft, almost porcelain-smooth skin, followed by the surrounding landscape and the two smaller figures, for which he used much more vigorous brush-strokes reminiscent of Impressionism. Because the landscape is entirely artificial, having been painted around the figures in the studio rather than out of doors, there is a certain lack of vitality, especially in the ripples on the water, which gives the painting a rather leaden, stiff appearance. The linear, classical emphasis of the nudes contrasts with the looser handling of the rest of the painting, but this may be an example of the sort of "irregularity" that Renoir was trying to achieve. The bright colours on the smooth white ground have also combined to give the painting an orange sheen, which may explain why this is sometimes known as Renoir's "sour" period. In many ways he was attempting too much in this work, and apart from Monet and one or two others who spoke favourably of it, the picture was not well received when it was exhibited at the Georges Petit gallery. It was eventually sold for 1000 francs to Jacques-Emile Blanche, a friend and fellow painter. The combination of his attempt to accommodate bourgeois taste and to emulate the example of the Old Masters had caused Renoir to paint an unhappy, unbalanced picture in which he was able neither to abandon the influence of Impressionism nor to submit fully to the discipline of traditional painting.

In this ambitious composition derived from the classical subjects of the Old Masters, Renoir was attempting to put on canvas some of the theories that had occupied him for the previous five years. He had developed a theory of "irregularism," which favoured a clear and structured composition but one that was not necessarily bound by rules of symmetry. At the same time he had absorbed the ideas of Impressionism, such as the light grounds and palette, and was unable to abandon them.

Nude Study
c 1886-7
Art Institute of Chicago

This chalk drawing is one of Renoir's many studies for *The Bathers*. In his earlier works of the 1860s and '70s he had painted his compositions straight onto the canvas, but in the 1880s he was concerned with capturing something of the monumental and classical feeling of Renaissance paintings. He was less than successful, as *The Bathers* neither lives up to the rigorous standards of traditional painting nor has the immediacy and freshness of Impressionism.

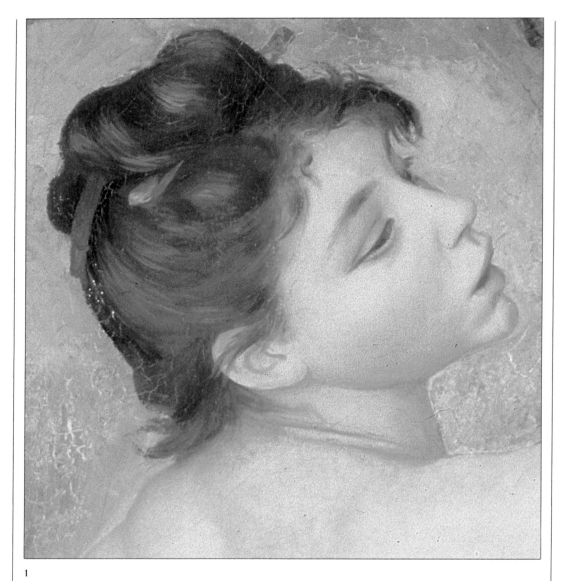

1

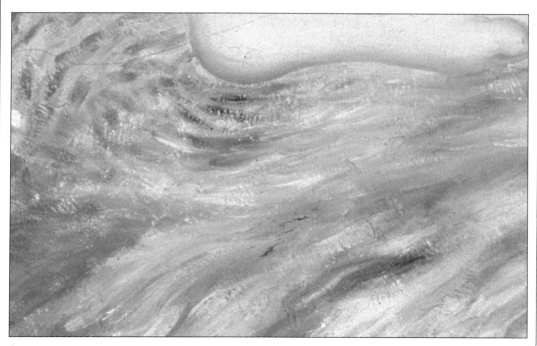

2

1 The head is the ultimate expression of Renoir's mannered, tight paintwork at this time. The brush-marks are barely visible, and the paint has been worked into an almost porcelain-like finish. The delicate lighting of the hair has been achieved from underneath by allowing the pale ground to limit the contour and shape, with orange worked on top in an attempt to give an impression of warmth and sunlight.

2 This detail shows the contrast between the harsh, academic style Renoir has used for the bodies and the freer use of paint and brushwork for the water. It also illustrates the studied artificiality of the work. Judging from the ripples of the water, the foot should be in contact with it, but in fact it appears to be floating free without any relationship with the water.

3 *Actual size detail* This detail also provides a contrast between the body of the nude, the towel and the background, each being painted in a different way. The skin of the arm is smoothly painted, with an orange glow that is presumably derived from the colour of the towel, but the towel itself seems solid and lifeless, with the folds rendered rather clumsily. The background is treated much more loosely and freely, its liveliness emphasizing the dullness of the towel.

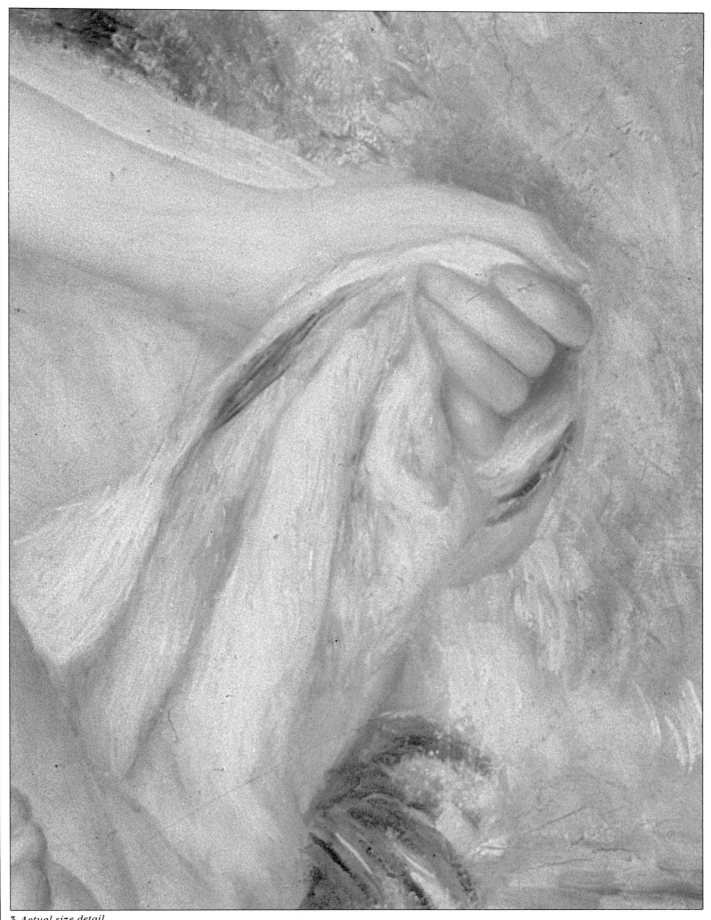

3 *Actual size detail*

GIRLS AT THE PIANO

(Jeunes Filles au Piano)
1892
45⅝×35½in/115.75×90.25cm
Oil on canvas
Musée d'Orsay, Paris

In 1892, through the influence of his friend, the poet Stéphane Mallarmé, Renoir received an official commission from the government. Mallarmé had been trying to persuade Henry Roujon, the new Director of Fine Arts, who wanted to buy a Renoir of the 1870s, that it would be better to commission a new work. Roujon finally agreed, and the picture, destined to enter the collection of the Luxembourg Palace specially devoted to the work of living artists, was *Girls at the Piano*.

Renoir was very excited by the commission and he set to work in great earnest, determined to produce the best he was capable of. The critic Arsène Alexandre, writing in the 1920s, recalled the circumstances of the commission and execution of the painting. "I remember the infinite pains he took in executing the official commission which a well-meaning friend had taken the trouble to gain for him. This was the young girls at the piano, a painting delicate and subtle in its execution, though its colour has yellowed somewhat. Renoir began this painting five or six times, each time almost identically; the idea of a commission was enough to paralyse him and to undermine his self-confidence. Tired of the struggle, he finally delivered to the Beaux Arts the picture which is today at the Museum, which immediately afterwards he adjudged the least good of the five or six." Renoir was paid 4,000 francs for the painting, with which he was well pleased, although controversy over which was the best of the several versions continued for some time.

All the works are very similar, with only minor compositional differences, and it is really only a matter of taste as to which is the best. The painting illustrated has a finesse and delicacy which hark back to the 1870s and show that Renoir had emerged from the stylistic and compositional traumas of the 1880s with his style and handling sure and confident. He was to stay with this new, tempered Impressionism until nearly the end of his life, when the restrictions caused by his arthritis forced a change in style.

In order to make the composition consistent from one version to the next, Renoir used tracing paper to transfer the figures rather than re-drawing the same figures freehand each time. Since the 1870s blue had no longer appeared in his shadows — very much a technique of Impressionism — and the shadows here are much warmer, using instead oranges and yellows. The paint is thinner than in the 1870s but not so dry or smooth as in *The Bathers* (see page 47), although the highlights on the clothes and the brackets on the piano have been painted quite thickly. A longer, more curvaceous brush-stroke has been used in the hair and clothes to create a more intimate rounded impression.

Before going on view at the Luxembourg, which was currently being restored, *Girls at the Piano* was loaned to Durand-Ruel for a one-man exhibition of Renoir's work. Mallarmé wrote to Roujon while it was on view there, "As for myself, and according to the unanimous impression gathered from all sides, I could not congratulate you enough for having chosen for a museum this definitive canvas, so calm and so free, a work of maturity. I see it once the dampness is gone and the painting is done, after a few months, like a feast in the Luxembourg, and completely accessible to visitors." In November the painting was formally admitted to the museum, marking Renoir's final arrival as an established modern painter. The stamp of official patronage ensured him from now on a steady flow of buyers and commissions.

Through his friend Stéphane Mallarmé, Renoir was commissioned by the Director of Fine Arts to produce a painting for the French state, to be hung in the Luxembourg Palace, demonstrating that he had at last gained official recognition for his work. He chose a subject that would not be controversial and would appeal to the tastes of the affluent bourgeoisie, and he worked hard at the commission, painting several versions of *Girls at the Piano*, each almost identical to its predecessor. This is the version that was finally delivered to the museum, and Renoir is reputed to have immediately judged it the least good.

1

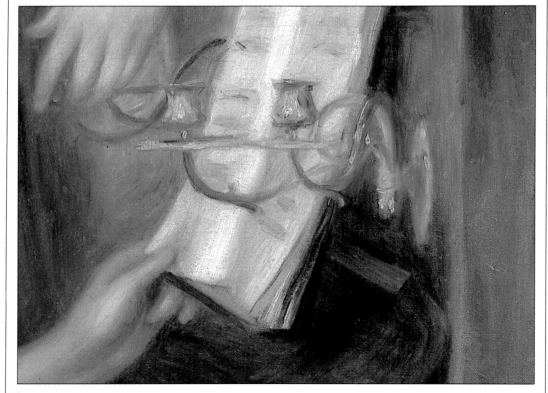

2

1 Renoir has used a rich array of colours for this work depicting a scene from comfortable bourgeois life. Gone are his earlier blues; these colours are warm and glowing, with the gold of the cushions and the girl's hair split by a wonderful pink on the sleeve of the other girl. The brush-strokes are long and worked to a smooth finish, probably in part due to his desire to please his "establishment" patrons.

2 The brass candle bracket has been swiftly highlighted in yellow, the paint applied on top of a duller yellow outlining. This gives the object a feeling of form and solidity as well as suggesting the hard, shiny qualities of the material itself.

3 *Actual size detail* The features of the young girl's face have been drawn very finely, with soft, smooth brushwork, while the golden hair and white collar show slightly broader strokes. This contrast of brushwork brings out the delicacy of the skin, with the gentle shadows under the chin and the fine pink bloom of the cheek.

3 *Actual size detail*

PORTRAIT OF MISIA

1904
36¼×28¾in/92×73cm
Oil on canvas
National Gallery, London

Misia Godebska was one of the great society beauties of turn-of-the-century Paris. She was much sought after as a model by painters such as Pierre Bonnard, Edouard Vuillard, Toulouse-Lautrec and Félix Vallotton as well as by Renoir, who painted her at least four times. She was married three times, firstly to Thadée Natanson, then to Albert Edwards and finally to José Maria Sert. At the time of this portrait she was still married to her first husband, who with his two brothers had founded the journal *La Revue blanche*. Misia's salon was much frequented by many of the young painters and writers, especially the painters of the Nabis school.

By 1904, when this portrait was painted, Jean Renoir, the artist's son, was beginning to watch his father at work, and he has left an interesting account in his book *Renoir My Father*: "I also mention the coat of silver white which he applied to the canvas before starting to add colour. He would ask the model posing for him, or whichever of his sons had been given the task, to increase the proportion of linseed oil. As a result the white took several days to dry; but it gave Renoir a smoother surface to work on. He did not like fine-grained canvases which were softer to paint on, for he thought them less resistant. In addition to this practical reason there was perhaps another one which was unconscious: his admiration for Veronese, Titian and Velasquez, who, it appears, painted on rather coarse-grained canvas. These reasons were complementary for my father was sure that the great masters wanted to produce work that would be lasting...I often prepared my father's canvases with flake white mixed with one third linseed oil and two thirds turpentine.It was then left to dry for several days." This portrait of Misia shows clearly the white ground shining through, which gives the work its fine luminous appearance.

Jean goes on to describe the actual application of the paint. "Renoir began by putting incomprehensible little touches on the white background, without even a suggestion of form. At times the paint, diluted with linseed oil and turpentine, was so liquid that it ran down the canvas. Renoir called it 'juice.' Thanks to the juice, he could, with several brush-strokes, establish the general tonality he was trying for. It covered almost the whole surface of the canvas...The background had to be very clear and smooth...He would begin with little pink or blue strokes, which would then be intermingled with burnt sienna, all perfectly balanced. As a rule Naples yellow and madder red were applied in the later stages. Ivory black came last of all. He next proceeded by direct or angular strokes. His method was round, so to speak, and in curves, as if he were following the contours of a young breast."

It is interesting to read this first-hand account of Renoir at work in the context of the finished portrait, where one can see the curvaceous quality of the brushwork and the gradual building up of the painting to finish with the yellows, reds and black that give it so much of its vibrancy. But the care with which Renoir prepared his canvases was not simply a matter of pictorial effect; he also had a deep concern for preserving the quality of the paint, regarding himself as a craftsman above all else. As Jean writes, "His concern for durability had nothing to do with the pride of believing his work worthy of eternity."

The sitter for this portrait, born Misia Godebska and of Russo-Polish extraction, was the wife of the journalist Thadée Nathanson. Later, she married an Englishman, Albert Edwards, and finally the Surrealist and Dada poet and painter José Maria Sert. At the time of this portrait she was a society beauty and the toast of intellectual and artistic Paris. She was much painted: Renoir himself did several portraits of her, as did other young artists whose work was championed by Nathanson through his literary and artistic journal *La Revue Blanche.*

1

2

1 A deliberate lack of close-up definition has been created by the warm shadows that rebound from one to the other between the face and fingers of the sitter. The ring has been painted very swiftly with several short, sharp strokes of black, and then given solidity by the simple device of one small stroke of white highlight.

2 The side of the sofa blends its warm colours into the shadows on the folds of the sitter's dress, which in turn throws some of its own colour back onto the sofa.

3 *Actual size detail* This detail shows the thinness of the paint, which has been mixed with turpentine to give greater fluidity. The pale ground has been allowed to show through, giving extra light and warmth to the painting, even where the colours are sombre. This can be seen most clearly in the bow, where the underpaint has given a warm luminosity even to black, the coldest of all colours.

3 *Actual size detail*

LES GRANDES BAIGNEUSES

1918-19
43¼×63in/109.75×160cm
Oil on canvas
Musée d'Orsay, Paris

This was Renoir's last large-scale master-piece, and one which recapitulated and summed up the ideas of the preceding few years. It borrows some of the compositional structure of the earlier work, *The Bathers* (see page 47), but is less awkward in appearance, and the classical motif has been treated with a much looser and more impressionistic brush-stroke reminiscent of the works of the early 1870s. Jean Renoir writes of this work that, "He felt that in this picture he had summed up all his researches and prepared a springboard from which he could plunge into further researches." Sadly, Renoir died before he was able to use his self-made springboard.

The immediate inspiration for the painting was reputedly the signing of the armistice on November 11, 1918, and it was painted through the winter of 1918-19. Jean Renoir has once again given some detailed descriptions which give an interesting insight into Renoir's palette. "Towards the end of his life he simplified his palette still further. Here, as nearly as I can remember, is the way he arranged his paints on his palette when he painted *Les Grandes Baigneuses*, now in the Louvre, in his studio in Cagnes. Starting on the lower side, next to the hole for his thumb; silver-white in a thick sausage-roll; Naples yellow in a small dot; and the same for the following colours: yellow ochre, sienna earth, red ochre; madder red, green earth, Veronese green, cobalt blue, ivory black. His choice of colours was not inflexible. On rare occasions I saw Renoir use Chinese vermilion, which he placed between the madder red and the green earth. In his final years he simplified his colour range still more and for certain pictures omitted either red ochre or green earth. Neither Gabrielle nor I ever saw him use chrome yellow. His economy of means was very impressive."

It must be remembered that when Renoir painted this work he was a very sick man. His hands were entirely crippled by arthritis and he was suffering with severe bronchial problems as well as being almost paralysed in his legs. In order for him to paint, Gabrielle or one of his sons had to prepare the palette and then force the brush between his fingers. This accounts for the much wider brush-strokes which delineate the forms and allow the warm priming and coarse canvas to show through. His paint was much thinned with turpentine, which greatly facilitated application but also caused the paints to run on the canvas; this can be seen particularly in the lower corners of the painting. The fiery colours and brightness of the paint make up for some of the unsurprising defects in technique, for the nudes have a lumpy, unnatural appearance and their bodies are rather unresolved. The landscape, like that in *The Bathers* of 1887, was painted indoors, which contributes to the air of artificiality in the work. But despite all the many handicaps, Renoir still loved the work he was doing, and his dedication has contrived to produce a painting of enormous strength, one which captivates the viewer with a sense almost of bewilderment at the beauty and fruitfulness of nature. It is a great irony that as Renoir the man was slowly but surely declining into death, Renoir the painter was leaping forward to new heights.

Renoir was inspired to paint this, his last major work, by the signing of the Armistice which brought World War One to a close on November 11, 1918. He was now over seventy-five and severely crippled with arthritis, but in spite of his suffering he has managed to create a work of enormous power. The composition is based on classical subject matter, but the flattened perspective and expressive brushwork both demonstrate Renoir's unabating search for new pictorial possibilities.

1

1 By this time Renoir's arthritis made it difficult for him to manipulate his brushes, and the paint has been much thinned with turpentine; the coarse texture of the canvas can be seen clearly beneath it. Small touches of slightly thicker paint have been used for the highlights on the bodies and the light froth of water, while the area of foliage between the figures shows touches of near-impasto in subtly glowing pinks and yellow-greens.

2 The thinning of the paint with turpentine has caused it to run in places, particularly in the reds of the blanket. Despite the increasing stiffness of his brush-strokes, Renoir has lost none of his brilliance of colour, which is notable in the golden straw of the hat and the deep pink of the rose.

3 *Actual size detail* The modelling of the face seems to tend towards an exaggerated roundness, giving the cheeks and mouth a rather distorted appearance. Renoir has used a pinkish priming, which strengthens the colours of the face and has given the hair an almost auburn glow in spite of the black paint he has used.

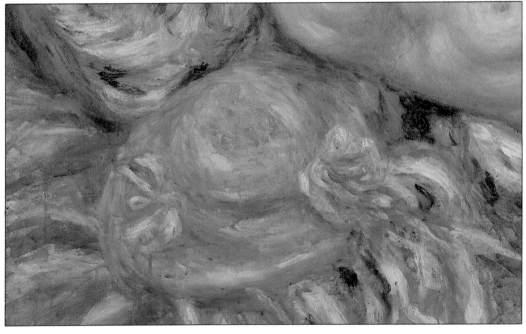

2

3 *Actual size detail*

Index

Page numbers in *italic* refer to illustrations and captions

A

academic painting, 16, *48*
Alexandre, Arsène, 50
André, Albert, 12

B

backgrounds, 20, 24, *26*, 34, *36*, *40*, 42, *48*, 54
Ball at the Moulin de la Galette, The, 12, 14, 28, *29-33*, 34, *35*
Barbizon school, 7
Bathers, The, 12, 46, *47-9*, 50, 58
Baudelaire, Charles, 20, *21*
Bazille, Frédéric, 7, 8, *9*, 10, 14, 16
  Still Life with Heron, 9
Blanche, Jacques-Emile, 46
Bonnard, Pierre, 54
Boucher, François, 6, 12
  Diana at the Bath, 7
Boudin, Eugène, 7
Bougival, 16
Box at the Theatre, The, *11*, 14, 20, *21-3*, 24, *25*

C

Café Guerbois, 14
Cagnes, 13, 14, 58
Caillebotte, Gustave, 14, 28, 34
canvases, 13
  fine-grained, 54
  priming, 9, 11, 16, 20, 24, 34, 42, *44*, 58
  ready prepared, 8, 16
  stretching, 9
  texture, *60*
Cézanne, Paul, 10, 12, 34
Charigot, Aline, 12, *13*, 14, 42

Charpentier, Georges, 12, 14, 38, *39*
Charpentier, Mme, 12, 13, 14, 38, *39-41*
Chocquet, Victor, 10, 12, 14, 38
classical subjects, 7, 10, 46, *47*, 58, *59*
Collettes, Les, 14, 58
colours, 13, *32*, 34, *44*, *48*, 50, *52*, 54, *56*, 58, *60*
  Barbizon school, 7, 8
  contrasts, 20, *21-2*, 26
  Courbet, 7, 8
  harmony, 34
  impasto, 20, 34, *60*
  Impressionists, 9, *21*, *35*, 38, 46, *47*
  machine-ground, 8
  merging, 16, *40*
  mixing, 28, *30*, *39*, 42
  palettes, 6, 7, *11*, 24, *25*, 38, *47*, 58
  patchwork effect, *36*
  reflected, 20
  relationships, 11, 34
  spectrum, *30*
composition, 20, *22*, 24, *25*, 34, 38, 42, 46, *47*, 50, *59*
Courbet, Gustave, 7, 8, 14

D

Dancer, The, 14, 24, *25-7*, 28
Degas, Edgar, 6, 14, 24, *25*
Delacroix, Eugène, 12
Deudon, Charles, 24
Diana, 7, 10
Diaz de la Peña, Narcisse Virgile, 7, 8
drawings, 6, 12, 34, 46, *47*, *50*
Durand-Ruel, Paul, 10, 12, 14, 24, *25*, 42, 46, 50

F

female nudes, 12, 46, *47-9*, 58, *59-61*
Fontainebleau, forest of, 7, 8
Fragonard, Jean Honoré, 6, 12, 34, *35*
  Bathers, The, 7
France, 6, 20
Franco-Prussian War, 10, 14
Frédéric Bazille at his Easel, 9

G

Gauguin, Paul, 12
Girls at the Piano, 14, 50, *51-3*
Gleyre, Charles, 7, 8, 14
Goenuette, Norbert, 28, 34
Gounod, Charles, 6
Grandes Baigneuses, Les, *11*, 14, 58, *59-61*
Genouillère, La, 8, *11*, 14, 16, *17-19*, 20
grounds, 8, 9, *11*, 16, 20, 24, 28, 34, *40*, 46, *47-8*, 54, 56

H

highlights, 16, 20, *22*, 24, 28, *32*, 34, *56*, *60*

I

impasto, 20, 34, *60*
Impressionists, 6, 8, 9, 10, *10*, 11, 12, 13, 14, 16, 20, *21*, 24, *25*, 28, *35-6*, 38, *39*, *43*, 46, *47*, 50, 58
Ingres, Jean Auguste Dominique, 12, 46
Italy, 12, 14, 42, *43*, 46

J

Jongkind, Johan, 7

L

landscapes, 6, *7*, 8, *10*, 12, 16, 20, 42, 46, 58
Lane, Sir Hugh, 42
Legrand, Alphonse, 24
Legrand, Marguerite, 28, 34
Legrand, Ninette, 24
Leroy, Louis, 24
Lévy frères, 14
light, *44*
   Impressionists, 6, 16, 46
   luminosity, 9, 16, 24, 34, 42, 54
   reflected, 20
Limoges, 6, 14
line, 16, *25*, 34, 42, 46

M

Mallarmé, Stéphane, 50, *51*
Manet, Edouard, 6, 8, *10*, 14
   Fife-player, The, 24, *25*
Michelangelo, 46
Mme Charpentier and her Children, 12, 13, 14, 38, *39-41*
modelling, *26, 40*, 42
Monet, Claude, 6, *7*, 8, *9*, 10, 12, 13, 14, 16, 20, 46
   Grenouillère, La, 8, 16, *17, 18*
   Impression, Sunrise, 24
Montmartre, 28, *29*, 35
Morisot, Berthe, 10

N

Nadar, *25*
Natanson, Misia, 14, *54, 55-7*

Nini, 20
Nude Study, 47

O

Old Masters, 6, 7, 11, 12, 20, 46, *47*
open-air painting, 7, 8, *11*, 12, 16, 20

P

palettes, 6, 7, *11*, 13, 16, 24, *25*, 38, *47*, 58
palette knife, *7*, 8
Paris, 8, *10*, 14, 16, *17*, 28, 54, *55*
Paris Commune, 10, 14
Père Martin, 20
perspective, 10, 16, 28, 38, 42, *59*
Petit, Georges, 12, 46
photography, 8, 10, *10*
Pissarro, Camille, 6, 8, 10, 12, 14, 20, 38
Pont des Arts, The, 8, *10*
Portrait of Misia, 54, *55-7*
portraits, 12, 13
   self-portrait, *6*
priming, 9, 11, 16, 20, 24, 34, 42, *44*, 58

R

Raphael, 46
Renaissance, 12, *47*
Renoir, Claude and Pierre, 12, *13*, 14
Renoir, Edmond, 20, 28, 34, 38
Renoir, Jean, 12, 13, *13*, 14, 34, 54, 58
Renoir, Léonard, 6, 14
Renoir, Pierre-Auguste,

background and early life, 6
influences on, 6, 7, *7*, 8, 10, *10*, 11, 12, 13, 34, *35*
painting methods, 8, 9, *9*, 11, *11*, 13, 24
patronage, 10
porcelain painter, 6, 7, 11, 13, 14
"sour period," 46
theory of "irregularism," 46, *47*
Roujon, Henri, 50

S

Salon, *7*, 8, 10, 12, 14, 38, *39*
Self-portrait, 6
Sert, José Maria, 54, *55*
shadows, 11, 20, *22*, 24, *26*, 34, *35, 44*, 50, *56*
Sisley, Alfred, 6, 7, 8, 10, 12, 14
sketches, 16, 28, *29*
Swing, The, 14, 34, *35-7*, 38, *39*

T U

Titian, 54
tones, 9, 13, 20, *22*, 24, 28, 54
Toulouse-Lautrec, Henri de, 54
Trehot, Lise, 14
Trouville, 16
Umbrellas, The, 11, 12, 14, 42, *43-5*
underpainting, *56*

V

Vallotton, Félix, 54
Velazquez, 54

Veronese, 54
Vidal de Solares y Cardeñas, Don Pedro, 28
Vollard, Ambroise, 12
Vuillard, Edouard, 54

W

wet-into-wet, 8, *11*, 16, *18*, 20, *26*, 28, *32, 39*, 42
Whitney, Mrs John Hay, 28

Z

Zola, Emile, 14

PHOTOGRAPHIC CREDITS

Barnes Foundation, Menon, Pennsylvania 13; Courtauld Institute
Galleries, London 21-23; Fogg Art Museum, Cambridge, Mass. 6;
Hubert Josse, Paris 9, 29-33, 35-37, 51-53, 59-61; Metropolitan
Museum of Art, New York 39-41; National Gallery, London 43-45;
55-57; National Gallery of Art, Washington 7 bottom; 25-27;
National Museum, Stockholm 17-19; Norton Simon Foundation, Los
Angeles 10; Philadelphia Museum of Art 47-49; Service
photographique de la Réunion des musées nationaux, Paris 7 top